SCHOLASTIC

Reading Passages
That Build Comprehension

PREDICTING

BY LINDA WARD BEECH

NEW YORK • TORONTO • LONDON • AUCKLAND • SYDNEY
MEXICO CITY • NEW DELHI • HONG KONG • BUENOS AIRES

Teaching
Resources

D1417967

Contents

Cover design by Maria Lilja
Interior design by Holly Grundon
Interior art by Mike Gordon

ISBN 0-439-55423-3
Copyright © 2005 by Linda Ward Beech.
All rights reserved.
Printed in the U.S.A.

8 9 10   40   14 13 12 11

Introduction

R eading comprehension involves numerous thinking skills. Making predictions is one such skill. A reader who can think ahead to determine what may happen next or how an event may turn out gains a richer understanding of a text. This book will help you help students learn to make reasonable predictions and anticipate probabilities. Use the pages that follow to teach this skill to students and to give them practice in employing it.

Using This Book

Pages 5-7

After introducing prediction to students (see page 4), duplicate and pass out pages 5–7. Use page 5 to help students review and practice what they have just learned about making predictions. By explaining their thinking, students are using metacognition to analyze how they made their predictions. Pages 6–7 give students a model of the practice pages to come. They also provide a model of the thinking students might use in making predictions.

Page 8

Use this page as a pre-assessment to find out how students think when they make predictions. When going over these pages with students, point out that a prediction is what is most likely to happen next. A prediction is formed using the information given and what the reader knows. A prediction makes sense.

Pages 9-43

These pages offer practice in making predictions. The first paragraph on each page is a nonfiction passage similar to one students might encounter in a social studies or science text. The second paragraph is a fictionalized passage similar to one they might find in a novel. After reading each paragraph, students should fill in the bubble in front of the correct answer for each question.

Pages 44-46

After they have completed the practice pages, use these pages to assess the way students think when they make predictions.

Page 47

You may wish to keep a record of students' progress as they complete the practice pages. Sample comments that will help you guide students toward improving their skills might include:
- reads carelessly
- misunderstands text
- fails to identify probabilities
- doesn't apply prior knowledge
- lacks background to make correct predictions

Teacher Tip

For students who need extra help, you might suggest that they keep pages 5–7 with them to use as examples when they complete the practice pages.

Mini-Lesson:
Teaching About Prediction

1. Introduce the concept: Write this sentence on the chalkboard:

The weather forecast is for rain.

Ask students which of the following sentences best suggests what will happen next.

○ A. Winston will take his umbrella to school.

○ B. Winston will leave his umbrella at home.

Teacher Tip

Students can learn a lot if you review the finished practice pages with them on a regular basis. Encourage students to explain their thinking for each correct answer. Ask them to point out the words that helped them figure out what might happen next. Discuss why the other sentences are not correct choices.

2. Model thinking: After students have correctly identified **A** as the sentence that best suggests what will happen, explore why by modeling how they might think aloud.

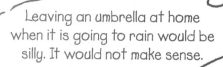

You listen to the weather forecast to find out what the weather will be like. That way you can dress and prepare yourself for the weather to come. If it is going to rain, an umbrella would be a good way to prepare for the weather.

Leaving an umbrella at home when it is going to rain would be silly. It would not make sense.

3. Define the skill: Explain to students that often a reader can use information in a text to think about what might happen next. Sometimes a reader considers information that he or she already knows to help guess what will happen. When a reader thinks about what will probably happen, he or she is making a **prediction**.

Information in the Text
It is going to rain.

What the Reader Knows
An umbrella is useful in the rain.

4. Practice the skill: Use Practice Pages 9–43 to give students practice in making predictions.

What Is a Prediction?

You read a passage. It gives you some information. But how will you use this information? A good reader thinks about the information. A reader might think:

What might happen next?

What is someone likely to do or feel?

As you answer these questions, you are making **predictions**. A prediction is a good guess about what will happen next.

Read the paragraph below, and then answer the questions.

Kevin's Book

Kevin read a book he liked a lot. He was really sorry when the story ended. He thought the author had done a great job. The next day Kevin took the book back to the library.

What facts are given in this paragraph?

1. What did Kevin think about the book?

   _____

2. How did Kevin feel when he finished the book?

   _____

3. What did Kevin think about the author?

   _____

Make a prediction.

4. What author might Kevin look for when he borrows another book from the library?

   _____

5. Why do you think so?

   _____

6. Have you ever done this?

   _____

When you make a prediction, use the information that is given. Use what you know as well. Put the information together. Ask yourself whether your prediction makes sense.

Name _____ Date _____

Making Predictions

Study these two pages. They show how a student made predictions.

Read the paragraph. Then fill in the
bubble that best answers the question.

Call 9-1-1

In an emergency people need help right away. Many towns use computer maps for emergency aid. When a 9-1-1 call comes in, the dispatcher looks at the computer map. It shows where the call is coming from. The dispatcher plots the fastest route to that place. This allows firefighters and ambulance drivers to get to a scene more quickly.

Which sentence tells what most likely happens next?

○ A. Ambulance drivers get lost.

This doesn't make sense. The maps help the dispatchers plot the routes.

● B. Injured people get to hospitals faster.

If an ambulance gets to an injured person faster, then it can get that person to a hospital faster.

○ C. People in trouble wait longer for help.

The paragraph says help gets there fast, so this isn't likely.

I am going to fill in **B.** This sentence is the best prediction of what might happen next.

Making Predictions

Thinking Model & Practice

Read the paragraph. Then fill in the
bubble that best answers the question.

Late Laura

Laura went to bed late and forgot to set her alarm. The next day she got up late. She had to rush to get to school. In her haste she left her homework on the kitchen table. At lunchtime she had to stay in and do it all over again.

Which sentence tells what most likely happens next?

○ A. Laura will set her
alarm the next night.

○ C. Laura won't do her
homework for the next day.

*This makes sense to me.
That's what I would do!*

*Nothing in the paragraph
suggests that Laura won't do her
homework. I don't think she is
looking for trouble.*

○ B. Laura will forget her
homework again.

*Students try not to do this two
days in a row. Who wants to stay
in at lunchtime?*

*I am going to choose **A.**
This prediction makes the most
sense to me.*

Name_____ Date_____

Thinking About What Will Happen

Read each sentence beginning. Choose the best sentence ending.

1. If you step in gum, your shoe will most likely get
   - ○ A. slippery.
   - ○ B. sticky.
   - ○ C. cold.

2. If you put water on a tissue, it will most likely get
   - ○ A. hard.
   - ○ B. smelly.
   - ○ C. soggy.

3. If you leave ice cream in the sun, it will most likely
   - ○ A. freeze.
   - ○ B. melt.
   - ○ C. harden.

4. If you blow on a candle, the flame will most likely
   - ○ A. go out.
   - ○ B. burn brighter.
   - ○ C. burn longer.

5. If you bump into someone, that person will most likely be
   - ○ A. curious.
   - ○ B. honored.
   - ○ C. annoyed.

6. If you do well on a test, you will most likely feel
   - ○ A. sad.
   - ○ B. proud.
   - ○ C. welcome.

7. If the lights in a theater dim, it most likely means
   - ○ A. a movie will begin.
   - ○ B. electricity is failing.
   - ○ C. a movie is over.

8. If you get stung by a bee, you will most likely feel
   - ○ A. shy.
   - ○ B. pain.
   - ○ C. happy.

Practice Page 1

Name_____ Date_____

Read each paragraph. Then fill in the bubble
that best answers each question.

A California Story

California is the raisin capital of the world. Farmers there begin by growing grapes. When the grapes are ripe, workers pick them from the vine. Then the grapes are laid out in California's dry, sunny air. The grapes begin to get wrinkled as they lose their water. They change color, too.

1. **Which sentence tells what most likely happens next?**

   ○ A. The grapes get moldy and rotten.

   ○ B. Farmers water the dry grapes.

   ○ C. The grapes turn into brown raisins.

Frank's Bike Ride

Frank has moved to a new town. He does not know his way around the neighborhood very well. Today he went for a bike ride. He had such a good time exploring that he didn't note all the turns he made. Now Frank is lost!

2. **Which sentence tells what most likely happens next?**

   ○ A. Frank will fall off his bike.

   ○ B. Frank will ask for directions.

   ○ C. Frank will keep on exploring.

Practice Page 2

Name_____ Date_____

Read each paragraph. Then fill in the bubble
that best answers each question.

The Snowshoe Hare

Animals of the Arctic
have different ways of
staying safe. Each summer the
snowshoe hare's fur is brown.
It is hard for enemies to see
the hare on the brown land
of the Arctic. But winter is
coming. It will soon snow. The
hare's thick fur will change
color to help keep it safe.

1. **Which sentence tells what most likely happens next?**

   ○ A. The hare's coat will become white.

   ○ B. The hare's enemies will see it in the snow.

   ○ C. The Arctic snow will turn brown.

The Spelling Bee

The spelling bee was almost
over. Only Peggy and Tony
were left. When it was Tony's turn,
he spelled M-A-G-A-Z-I-N-E
correctly. Then it was Peggy's turn.
The word was S-I-T-U-A-T-I-O-N.
Peggy did not know how to spell it.
Tony did.

2. **Which sentence tells what most likely happens next?**

   ○ A. Peggy will win the spelling bee.

   ○ B. Tony will help Peggy spell the word.

   ○ C. Tony will win the spelling bee.

Name_____   Date_____

Read each paragraph. Then fill in the bubble
that best answers each question.

In a Supermarket

A supermarket makes more money on some things than others. So money-making items are placed where shoppers will see them. For example, special buns may be on a table in the front. However, milk and butter are in the back of the store. These are things that people almost always buy. A shopper who needs milk passes lots of tempting things on the way to the back of the store.

1. **Which sentence tells what most likely happens next?**

   ○ A. A shopper will buy only a carton of milk.

   ○ B. A shopper will buy milk and something else.

   ○ C. A shopper will forget to buy milk.

Juan and the Watch

Juan found a watch in front of a neighbor's apartment. He took the watch to the neighbors. They were very grateful to get their watch. They gave Juan a reward.

2. **Which sentence tells what most likely happens next?**

   ○ A. Juan will look for other watches.

   ○ B. Juan will thank the neighbors.

   ○ C. Juan will ask for the watch.

Practice Page **4**

Name_____ Date_____

Read each paragraph. Then fill in the bubble
that best answers each question.

Measuring the Wind

The Beaufort scale tells how hard the wind is blowing. A calm day is 0 on the scale. The wind blows less than one mile an hour. A 3 on the scale means winds of up to 12 miles an hour. Umbrellas are hard to use when the wind's scale is 6. It isn't easy to walk in the wind when the scale is 7. But today the wind is up to 10. Watch out!

1. **Which sentence tells what most likely happens next?**

   ○ A. Many people will go hiking.

   ○ B. Leaves on trees will be still.

   ○ C. Whole trees may be uprooted.

Ted's Role

Ted has a role in the class play. He didn't do a good job of learning his lines. He didn't pay attention at rehearsals. Instead, he spent most of the time joking around. Today is the big performance. Everyone's parents are coming.

2. **Which sentence tells what most likely happens next?**

   ○ A. Ted won't remember his lines.

   ○ B. Ted will get the most applause.

   ○ C. Ted's parents will be proud.

Practice Page 5

Name_____ Date_____

Read each paragraph. Then fill in the bubble
that best answers each question.

Long-Ago Pumpkins

In the 1600s Native Americans such as the Pequot planted pumpkins in their cornfields. The big pumpkin leaves helped to keep the soil damp and free from weeds. Native Americans also used pumpkins for food and medicine. The English colonists were surprised. They thought pumpkins were only fit for animals. But the colonists had little food; they were hungry.

1. **Which sentence tells what most likely happens next?**
   ○ A. The colonists get sick from eating pumpkins.
   ○ B. The colonists begin to rise and eat pumpkins.
   ○ C. The Native Americans stop eating pumpkins.

Amy's Bill

Amy got her telephone bill. It told how much she owed. It also stated when payment was due. If Amy didn't pay the bill on time, there would be an extra charge. Amy wrote the date on her calendar. Then she put the bill on her desk.

2. **Which sentence tells what most likely happens next?**
   ○ A. Amy won't bother to pay her bill.
   ○ B. Amy will pay her phone bill on time.
   ○ C. Amy will pay her telephone bill late.

Practice Page 6

Name_____ Date_____

Read each paragraph. Then fill in the bubble
that best answers each question.

Different Customs

People everywhere follow different customs. It is a good idea for travelers to know what these are in the places they visit. In China it is the custom to give special foods to an honored guest. These include fish lips and fish eyes. Sometimes guests refuse such foods.

1. **Which sentence tells what most likely happens next?**

   ○ A. The Chinese will think their guests are rude.

   ○ B. The guests will ask for the fish eye recipe.

   ○ C. The Chinese will send out for pizza.

A Snowy Day

When Ellen wakes up on Saturday, there is snow on the ground. Ellen races through her breakfast. Then she pulls on a hat, jacket, and gloves. Her boots are not in the closet, so she runs outside in her sneakers. She joins her friends to go sledding.

2. **Which sentence tells what most likely happens next?**

   ○ A. Ellen's feet will get cold and wet.

   ○ B. Ellen will lose her sled on the hill.

   ○ C. Ellen's friends will take off their boots.

Practice Page 7

Name_____   Date_____

Read each paragraph. Then fill in the bubble
that best answers each question.

Pompeii

Long ago, people lived in a Roman city called Pompeii, in Italy. Then a nearby volcano erupted. Pompeii was completely covered. Hundreds of years later, scientists began to dig it out. Little by little they have been uncovering the ancient city. They have set up museums to display the things they have found.

1. **Which sentence tells what most likely happens next?**

   ○ A. The ancient people of Pompeii will come to life.

   ○ B. Scientists will give up working at Pompeii.

   ○ C. Scientists will continue learning about the past.

The Plane Contest

Jay and Chuck made paper airplanes. They decided to have a contest. Which plane could go the farthest? Jay went first. His plane glided well before it landed. Then Chuck sent up his plane. It didn't look as if it would go far. But suddenly a gust of wind came by. Chuck held his breath as his plane soared.

2. **Which sentence tells what most likely happens next?**

   ○ A. Jay's plane will crash into a tree.

   ○ B. Chuck's plane will go backward.

   ○ C. Chuck will win the plane contest.

Practice Page **8**

Name_____ Date_____

Read each paragraph. Then fill in the bubble
that best answers each question.

Paprika From Hungary

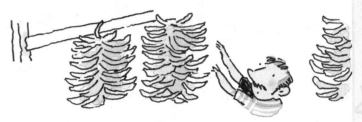

Hungary is known for its paprika. This red spice is used in cooking all over the world. Each fall the fields of Hungary are dotted with red plants. These are pepper plants. Once the peppers have been picked, they are hung on frames to dry. Then the dried peppers are ground into a fine powder. The peppers are now paprika.

1. **Which sentence tells what most likely happens next?**

   ◯ A. The paprika will be sold as a spice.

   ◯ B. The workers will all start to sneeze.

   ◯ C. The peppers will be sold for salads.

Bullet

Bullet is Barry's dog. Most days Bullet looks out the window at all the things he'd like to chase. When they go for a walk, Barry keeps Bullet on a leash. But today, while Barry was holding the door open for his Mom, Bullet slipped out.

2. **Which sentence tells what most likely happens next?**

   ◯ A. Bullet will wait for Barry to get his leash.

   ◯ B. Bullet will chase something in the yard.

   ◯ C. Barry's mother will praise Bullet.

Practice Page 9

Name_____ Date_____

Read each paragraph. Then fill in the bubble
that best answers each question.

Taking Zoo Photos

Jessie is a photographer.
Most of the time she works
in a zoo. She loves her job, but it
is not easy to get good pictures.
The animals do not know they
should stay still for a photo. So
Jessie has to wait for just the
right moment. Today Jessie is
taking shots of the orangutans.
They are her favorites. She
knows they can be very silly!

1. **Which sentence tells what most likely
   happens next?**

   ○ A. Jessie will yell at the orangutans.

   ○ B. The orangutans will sit quietly.

   ○ C. The orangutans will make
         funny faces.

The Rodeo

Steve went to the rodeo with
his father. It was a very
exciting day. Steve enjoyed the
crowds, odors, and sounds. He
loved the animals and the colorful
outfits of the riders. At school
Steve told his friends all about
the rodeo.

2. **Which sentence tells what most
   likely happens next?**

   ○ A. Steve will find out more
         about rodeos.

   ○ B. Steve will forget all about
         rodeos.

   ○ C. Steve's father will join
         the rodeo.

Name_____   Date_____

Read each paragraph. Then fill in the bubble that best answers each question.

Communicating

Once people used the smoke from bonfires to send messages over long distances. People built towers and used flags to send signals too. In the 1800s the telegraph was invented. In 1876 Alexander Graham Bell invented the first telephone. Today millions of people communicate with computers and cell phones. Staying in touch keeps getting faster and easier.

1. **Which sentence tells what most likely happens next?**

   ○ A. People will go back to sending messages by bonfires.

   ○ B. New ways of communicating will continue to develop.

   ○ C. People will get tired of so much communication all the time.

Garden Melons

Mr. Lewin planted some melons in his garden. He watered the plants as they grew. He pulled out weeds so the plants had plenty of room. Now the melons are almost ripe.

2. **Which sentence tells what most likely happens next?**

   ○ A. Mr. Lewin will pick the melons.

   ○ B. Mr. Lewin will cut the leaves off.

   ○ C. Mr. Lewin will go on vacation.

Practice Page 11   Name_____   Date_____

Read each paragraph. Then fill in the bubble that best answers each question.

Ladybugs

What do ladybugs eat? Their main food is a tiny insect called an aphid. Most gardeners think of aphids as pests. These insects cause harm to plants by sucking out their juices. When people see ladybugs in their gardens, however, they are pleased.

1. **Which sentence tells what most likely happens next?**

   ○ A. Gardeners will get rid of the ladybugs.

   ○ B. The ladybugs will eat the aphids.

   ○ C. The aphids will attack the ladybugs.

Bill's Visit

Bill is an actor. Many years ago he went to our school. Yesterday Bill came to visit the school. We were rehearsing a play. So Bill stayed to watch for a while. Later he asked our teacher if he could talk to us.

2. **Which sentence tells what most likely happens next?**

   ○ A. Bill will make fun of our play.

   ○ B. Bill will offer some tips to us.

   ○ C. Bill will ask to be in our play.

Practice Page 12

Name_____ Date_____

Read each paragraph. Then fill in the bubble that best answers each question.

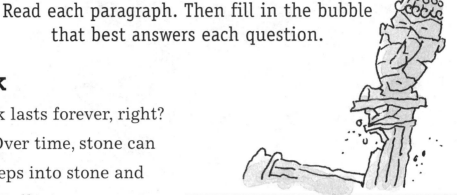

Stonework

Stonework lasts forever, right? Wrong. Over time, stone can decay. Frost seeps into stone and causes cracks. Pollution causes problems. So does acid rain. When a tree branch rubs against something made of stone, the stone begins to wear away. Today many fine old stone buildings are in bad shape. People spend a lot of time and money restoring them.

1. **Which sentence tells what most likely happens next?**

   ○ A. Builders will take down all stone buildings.

   ○ B. People will try to take better care of old stonework.

   ○ C. People will let old stonework fall apart.

Marie's Candy

Marie had some chocolate candies. She ate one and gave one to her friend Judy. Then the girls decided to play jump rope. Marie left the candy in the sun while they played.

2. **Which sentence tells what most likely happens next?**

   ○ A. The jump rope will get covered with chocolate.

   ○ B. The girls will slip in the chocolate.

   ○ C. The candies will melt in the sun.

Name_____ Date_____

Read each paragraph. Then fill in the bubble
that best answers each question.

Highway in a Park

A highway runs through a big park in Canada. The park is home to all sorts of wild animals. But the animals often cross the highway for food and water. Many are hurt or killed by cars and trucks. So park workers built bridges called overpasses, just for the animals. They put up fences along the highway on either side of the overpasses.

1. **Which sentence tells what most likely happens next?**

   ○ A. The animals will learn to use the overpasses.

   ○ B. The animals will jump over the fences.

   ○ C. The animals will go without food and water.

The Costume Party

Yuki was invited to a costume party. She wanted to go but didn't know what to wear. Her mom said she could not afford to buy a costume. Yuki looked through all the closets for ideas. Then she spotted some boots and poles.

2. **Which sentence tells what most likely happens next?**

   ○ A. Yuki will dress up as a skier.

   ○ B. Yuki will stay home from the party.

   ○ C. Yuki will borrow a friend's costume.

Practice Page 14

Name_____ Date_____

Read each paragraph. Then fill in the bubble
that best answers each question.

Space Junk

Did you know there is junk in space? This junk is made up of old satellites, rockets, and even tools lost by astronauts. Space junk can hit a spacecraft and damage it. Usually, scientists can guide a spacecraft away from space junk. But as more and more junk is left in space, the danger grows. So scientists are working on ideas for getting rid of space junk.

1. **Which sentence tells what most likely happens next?**

   ◯ A. Scientists will stop worrying about space junk.

   ◯ B. Space junk will start to fall to Earth.

   ◯ C. Scientists will find ways to clean up space.

Bert's Birthday

Sue knew that her brother Bert's birthday was coming soon. She wanted to buy him a gift. It was hard to decide what to get. One day Bert told Sue about a book he had read. It was about fish. Bert seemed really interested in this topic.

2. **Which sentence tells what most likely happens next?**

   ◯ A. Sue will serve fish for dinner on Bert's birthday.

   ◯ B. Sue will get Bert some goldfish for his birthday.

   ◯ C. Sue will forget to buy a present for Bert.

Practice Page 15

Name_____ Date_____

Read each paragraph. Then fill in the bubble
that best answers each question.

Special Days

Newfoundlands are a
special kind of dog.
They have layers of fat
under their skin and thick,
oily fur. They also have
webbed feet. Long ago,
fishermen used these dogs
to pull their fishing nets.
The Newfoundlands would
often dive in after fishermen
who fell overboard too.

1. **Which sentence tells what most likely happens next?**

   ○ A. People began using Newfoundlands as rescue dogs.

   ○ B. Newfoundlands began eating too much fish from the nets.

   ○ C. People thought Newfoundlands would be good house pets.

Tying Knots

Joan wanted to learn how to tie
knots. She got a book from the
library and read it carefully. She tried
to follow the directions. But Joan had a
hard time. Her knots did not always
come out right. Joan didn't give up
though. She kept working at those knots.

2. **Which sentence tells what most likely happens next?**

   ○ A. Joan will decide to learn another skill.

   ○ B. Joan will write to the book's author.

   ○ C. Joan will learn how to tie knots.

Name_____   Date_____

Read each paragraph. Then fill in the bubble
that best answers each question.

Flying South

Wild cranes fly south each fall. But cranes raised by people do not have parents to teach them how to do this. So scientists trained some cranes they had raised to follow a small plane. The pilot played a tape of adult cranes calling one another. Then the plane took off. The tame cranes followed it. The plane flew for two hours each day. So did the birds.

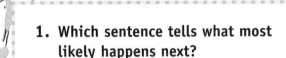

1. **Which sentence tells what most
likely happens next?**

   ○ A. The cranes will learn to fly
   south by themselves.

   ○ B. The cranes will get into the
   plane with the pilot.

   ○ C. Wild cranes will start to
   follow the plane too.

A Family Picnic

The Alanos went on a family picnic. They chose a pretty place to sit. It had a nice view of a pond. No one saw the anthill. Mr. Alano spread a blanket. Mrs. Alano took all the food from the basket. The family began to eat.

2. **Which sentence tells what most
likely happens next?**

   ○ A. Mr. Alano will fall in the pond.

   ○ B. Mrs. Alano will take a nap.

   ○ C. The ants will share the picnic.

Name_____ Date_____

Read each paragraph. Then fill in the bubble
that best answers each question.

Butterfly Travels

The monarch butterfly is quite a
traveler. Each spring the monarch
leaves Mexico. It starts flying north to
Canada. On the way, it dies.
But its young continue north.
These butterflies also die,
but their young go on. This
continues until fall. Then the
great-great-grandchild of
the first butterfly turns and
heads south.

1. **Which sentence tells what most likely
   happens next?**
   ○ A. The young butterfly will get lost.

   ○ B. The young butterfly will fly east.

   ○ C. The young butterfly will head
         for Mexico.

At the Beach

Lou and Len were at the
beach with their father. The
boys decided to make a fort in the
sand. They chose a place where
the sand was wet and easy to
work with. They worked for a
long time. Then they went for a
swim with their dad. Lou noticed
that the tide was coming in.

2. **Which sentence tells what most
   likely happens next?**
   ○ A. Some seagulls will attack the
         sand castle.

   ○ B. The boys' dad will jump on
         the sand castle.

   ○ C. The tide will wash away the
         sand castle.

Name_____ Date_____

Read each paragraph. Then fill in the bubble
that best answers each question.

A New Road

A bulldozer clears a path. Then a scraper makes the path smooth. A grader spreads the dirt to make the path even. Along comes a water truck to water the path. It is followed by a roller. Then more trucks drop loads of small stones to be pressed into the surface. Still another truck sprays tar on the path. Finally, sand is spread and rolled into the tar. A new road is ready.

1. **Which sentence tells what most likely happens next?**
   ○ A. Boats will begin traveling on the road.
   ○ B. The road will open to cars and trucks.
   ○ C. The road will be closed for repairs.

Dinner Plans

Mr. Kelly was invited to a friend's house for dinner after work. As he was putting on his coat, his office phone rang. The call took a while. It looked as if Mr. Kelly would be late for dinner.

2. **Which sentence tells what most likely happens next?**
   ○ A. Mr. Kelly will go home instead.
   ○ B. Mr. Kelly will call to say he'll be late.
   ○ C. Mr. Kelly will go without dinner tonight.

Practice Page 19

Name_____ Date_____

Read each paragraph. Then fill in the bubble
that best answers each question.

What Happened?

Millions of years ago, dinosaurs lived on Earth. Then they disappeared. What happened to them? Did they all get a disease? Were they too stupid to protect themselves from enemies? Did a huge asteroid crash into Earth and cause a giant cloud that blocked the sun? Did a super volcano on Earth blow up? No one is sure. But scientists keep coming up with possible ideas.

1. **Which sentence tells what most likely happens next?**

   ○ A. Scientists will keep working on the mystery.

   ○ B. Scientists will give up on solving the mystery.

   ○ C. Scientists will find some living dinosaurs.

The Race

Deedee is planning to run in a race this weekend. She has been working out for weeks to get ready. Today she slipped on a wet sidewalk covered with leaves. Now Deedee's ankle hurts. She can't put any weight on it.

2. **Which sentence tells what most likely happens next?**

   ○ A. Deedee will drop out of the race.

   ○ B. Deedee will have someone run for her.

   ○ C. Deedee will run in the race anyway.

Practice Page 20 Name_____ Date_____

Read each paragraph. Then fill in the bubble
that best answers each question.

Underground Water

Sometimes rainwater makes its way through small spaces in underground rock. This water may travel underground for thousands of years. Over time the water carves out caves in the rock. In some places underground rivers flow through the caves. The moving water wears away the cave walls and forms new passageways.

1. **Which sentence tells what most likely happens next?**

   ○ A. The water will disappear from the caves.

   ○ B. The water in the caves will begin to freeze.

   ○ C. The water will keep on changing the caves.

The Bird Feeder

Barb and her mother bought a bird feeder. They studied their yard to find a good place for it. When the feeder was set up, Barb filled it with birdseed. Then she and her mother began watching the feeder each morning.

2. **Which sentence tells what most likely happens next?**

   ○ A. Barb and her mother will eat the birdseed.

   ○ B. Barb and her mother will watch the birds eating.

   ○ C. Barb and her mother will take down the feeder.

Practice Page 21 Name_____ Date_____

Read each paragraph. Then fill in the bubble
that best answers each question.

Words, Words, Words

Will the word *muggles* soon
appear in a dictionary?
Words in the English language
keep changing. Sometimes people
stop using certain words. Very
often new words enter the
language. For example, *e-mail*
came into use with computers.
Dictionary writers keep busy
tracking these changes.

1. **Which sentence tells what most
   likely happens next?**

   ○ A. People will stop selling new
     dictionaries.

   ○ B. The words in dictionaries will
     keep changing.

   ○ C. The English language will run
     out of new words.

A Snowy Problem

It began to snow in the
afternoon. Mr. Burns watched
it cover his yard and sidewalk.
At about four o'clock the snow
stopped. Mr. Burns needed to go
to the store. But the snow in
front of his house was very deep.

2. **Which sentence tells what most
   likely happens next?**

   ○ A. Mr. Burns will shovel his
     sidewalk.

   ○ B. Mr. Burns will get out his sled.

   ○ C. Mr. Burns will wait for the snow
     to melt.

Practice Page **22**

Name_____ Date_____

Read each paragraph. Then fill in the bubble
that best answers each question.

Camping Equipment

Camping keeps getting easier. In 1923 the first gas camp stove was sold. Backpacks became lighter in the mid 1950s. That's when aluminum tubes were used in backpack frames. By 1976 campers could take freeze-dried foods on their outings. In the 1980s special lightweight hiking boots came out. And in the 1990s new tent designs were available.

1. **Which sentence tells what most likely happens next?**
   ○ A. Improved equipment will help campers.
   ○ B. People will give up hiking and camping.
   ○ C. Camping equipment will get harder to use.

Rita's Lunch

Rita bought a sandwich and a container of tea. As the clerk put Rita's things in a paper bag, the tea spilled a little. Neither Rita nor the clerk noticed. Then Rita headed for the park to eat her lunch.

2. **Which sentence tells what most likely happens next?**
   ○ A. The clerk will run after Rita with a dry bag.
   ○ B. Rita's lunch will fall through the wet bag.
   ○ C. Rita will enjoy her lunch in the park.

Practice Page 23

Name_____ Date_____

Read each paragraph. Then fill in the bubble
that best answers each question.

Robot Helpers

Robots have explored other planets. These machines also do many jobs in factories. For example, robots are used to make cars. People use robots to do dangerous work such as exploring volcanoes or the ocean floor. Robots are also used to give directions in shopping centers and amusement parks. Scientists keep finding more ways for robots to help us.

1. **Which sentence tells what most likely happens next?**

   ○ A. Robots will get tired of doing so much.

   ○ B. Robots will take over the world.

   ○ C. Many more uses will be found for robots.

A Catalog Call

Mrs. Rivers got a big catalog in the mail. She looked at all the different things there were to buy. A colorful dog bed caught her eye. It would be just the thing for her dog, Shep. So Mrs. Rivers called the catalog company.

2. **Which sentence tells what most likely happens next?**

   ○ A. Shep will pay for the dog bed.

   ○ B. The dog bed will be sent to Mrs. Rivers.

   ○ C. Mrs. Rivers will sleep in the dog bed.

Practice Page 24

Name_____   Date_____

Read each paragraph. Then fill in the bubble
that best answers each question.

A Special Museum

Have you read the picture book
The Very Hungry Caterpillar?
It is one of many books
written and drawn by Eric
Carle. In 2002 Mr. Carle
started a museum of picture
books. The museum shows the
art from different children's
books. After looking at a
picture, many children want
to read the book it came from.

1. **Which sentence tells what most likely happens next?**

   ○ A. The children will write a letter to the author asking for the book.

   ○ B. The children will find the book they want in the library.

   ○ C. The children will draw their own pictures on the museum wall.

After School

Clark was very hungry when
he came home from school.
His nose led him right to the
kitchen. Something there smelled
good! Sure enough, Clark saw his
older sister taking some cupcakes
out of the oven.

2. **Which sentence tells what most likely happens next?**

   ○ A. Clark's sister will drop the cupcakes.

   ○ B. Clark will ask his sister for a cupcake.

   ○ C. Clark will do his homework in the kitchen.

Name_____ Date_____

Read each paragraph. Then fill in the bubble
that best answers each question.

Firsts for Presidents

United States presidents like
to try new inventions. In
1833 Andrew Jackson was the
first president to ride on a train.
The first president to have his
photo taken was James Knox
Polk. That was in 1849. Theodore
Roosevelt was the first president
to ride in a car, and Warren G.
Harding was the first to be on the
radio. Who was the first president
on TV? It was Dwight Eisenhower.

1. **Which sentence tells what most
   likely happens next?**

   ○ A. Presidents will invent many
   new things.

   ○ B. Presidents will stop trying
   new things.

   ○ C. Presidents will keep on trying
   new things.

Niko's Trees

Niko and his dad were
looking at the trees in their
backyard. As the cool days of fall
began, the trees were turning
pretty colors. Niko loved the
bright red and yellow leaves. He
wished the trees would stay like
this and not change anymore.

2. **Which sentence tells what most
   likely happens next?**

   ○ A. The leaves will start to fall
   off the trees.

   ○ B. The leaves will turn green
   very soon.

   ○ C. Birds will start making nests
   in the trees.

Practice Page 26

Name_____ Date_____

Read each paragraph. Then fill in the bubble
that best answers each question.

Tricking the Brain

BLUE. You just read the word for the color blue. You read the words for colors all the time. But if the letters for BLUE are printed in the color green, it is harder for you to read the word. That's because your brain is getting two messages—blue and green. The brain gets confused when it receives two messages that don't agree. Suppose you see a sign that says RED. The letters are yellow.

1. **Which sentence tells what most likely happens next?**

   ○ A. Your brain will read the word ORANGE.

   ○ B. Your brain will read the word RED quickly.

   ○ C. Your brain will take longer to get the message.

Tessa's Room

Tessa has a messy room. Her books and games are scattered all over. Her clothes are in a heap on the floor. Tomorrow Tessa's grandmother is coming for a visit. Tessa's dad has come up to her room for a talk.

2. **Which sentence tells what most likely happens next?**

   ○ A. Tessa's dad will clean up the room.

   ○ B. Tessa's grandmother will visit another time.

   ○ C. Tessa's dad will tell Tessa to clean her room.

Practice Page 27

Name_____   Date_____

Read each paragraph. Then fill in the bubble
that best answers each question.

The Loch Ness Monster

Loch Ness is a large lake in Scotland. Many people think a huge monster lives in the lake. The stories first started in the year 565. At that time reports said that a lake monster killed a swimmer. Since then many people have told tales about the monster. Some people have even made fake photos of it. Scientists have made tests but cannot prove it is real—or unreal.

1. **Which sentence tells what most likely happens next?**

   ○ A. Loch Ness monster stories will continue.

   ○ B. People will stop believing in the monster.

   ○ C. The Loch Ness monster will come up on land.

Wildflowers

Holly went for a walk with her aunt and uncle. Along the way she picked some pretty wildflowers. Later they stopped to eat lunch on a rock by a stream. Holly was tired by the time they finally got home.

2. **Which sentence tells what most likely happens next?**

   ○ A. Holly will find that her wildflowers have wilted.

   ○ B. Holly will try to sell her wildflowers.

   ○ C. Holly will plant the wildflowers in her garden.

Practice Page **28**

Name_____ Date_____

Read each paragraph. Then fill in the bubble
that best answers each question.

Factory Visits

Many people like to see how things are made. Factories have found that visitors can be big business. For example, families drive many miles to visit factories that make crayons and baseball bats. Other popular factories with tours are places that make teddy bears, cereal, and chocolate bars. Many tours end with a question-and-answer period.

1. **Which sentence tells what most likely happens next?**

   ○ A. People will wait in line to take the tour again.

   ○ B. People will shop at the factory gift shop.

   ○ C. People will try to get jobs working at the factory.

Leon's Desk

Leon's desk is near a window. He often opens the window in the warm weather. Usually, he leaves it open during the night while he sleeps. This morning, as Leon gets up, he sees that it is raining.

2. **Which sentence tells what most likely happens next?**

   ○ A. Leon will open the window a little wider.

   ○ B. Leon will go back to bed until the rain stops.

   ○ C. Leon will find that his desk is wet.

Practice Page 29   Name_____   Date_____

Read each paragraph. Then fill in the bubble
that best answers each question.

Heat and Size

Some things get larger as they are heated. Gases are a good example. Gases are in the air. Most of the time you can't see them. Gases move around and have no shape of their own. When a gas inside a container warms up, the gas takes up more room. Put a balloon over the top of an empty plastic bottle. Place the bottle in a bowl of hot water.

1. Which sentence tells what most likely happens next?

○ A. The balloon will fall off the bottle.

○ B. The balloon will get bigger.

○ C. The balloon will change color.

The Wind

Kareem could hear the telephone ring as he got off the elevator. He opened the door and dashed for the phone. In his hurry he left the apartment door open. While Kareem was talking, a gust of air swept down the hallway of the building.

2. Which sentence tells what most likely happens next?

○ A. The wind will blow the apartment door shut.

○ B. The wind will blow the telephone off the wall.

○ C. The wind will blow leaves into the apartment.

Practice Page **30** Name_____ Date_____

Read each paragraph. Then fill in the bubble
that best answers each question.

Mirrors

People keep finding new uses for mirrors. People began looking at themselves in mirrors in ancient Egypt. In the 1870s the U.S. Army sent messages by flashing mirrors. Today California uses almost 2,000 mirrors to make electricity. A huge mirror in France collects enough heat from the sun to melt metal.

1. Which sentence tells what most likely happens next?

○ A. People will give up looking in mirrors.

○ B. Only magicians will continue to use mirrors.

○ C. Mirrors will be used in more new ways.

At the End

The play was in its last act. The actors said their final lines. Then the play was over. It was a good ending. The curtain went down, and the actors came out to take a bow.

2. Which sentence tells what most likely happens next?

○ A. The actors will sit in the audience.

○ B. The audience will clap for the actors.

○ C. The audience will act in the play.

Practice Page **31**

Name_____ Date_____

Read each paragraph. Then fill in the bubble
that best answers each question.

Magpie Problems

Magpies are large black-and-white birds. In Australia these birds are a problem. The magpies often swoop down on people who get too close to their nests. Sometimes the birds cause harm. In many places warning signs are posted. These signs say "Beware of Swooping Magpies." As a result, people know what to do when they see a magpie.

1. **Which sentence tells what most likely happens next?**

    ○ A. People will laugh at the warning signs.

    ○ B. The magpies will swoop down on the signs.

    ○ C. People will cover their heads and run.

Izzy and Ozzie

Izzy is always fooling around with his older brother, Ozzie. Their sister is always telling them to stop. But the boys think it is funny. At dinner tonight Ozzie starts making faces at Izzy. Izzy stands up and leans over his food to make faces at his brother.

2. **Which sentence tells what most likely happens next?**

    ○ A. The boys will listen to their sister.

    ○ B. Ozzie will tell Izzy to act his age.

    ○ C. Izzy will probably knock something over.

Practice Page 32

Name_____ Date_____

Read each paragraph. Then fill in the bubble
that best answers each question.

Heat and Color

Dark things absorb, or take in, heat more than others. That is why dark clothes seem hotter in the sun. Dark, shiny cars feel hotter too. Light colors reflect the sun's heat away. In hot countries people often paint their homes white to keep them cooler. As warm summer months approach, many people change the clothes in their closets.

1. **Which sentence tells what most likely happens next?**

   ○ A. People will start wearing light-colored clothes.

   ○ B. People will start wearing dark-colored clothes.

   ○ C. People will start painting their houses brown.

Doris Practices

Doris is a little short for her age. But she wants to play on the school basketball team. So Doris practices all the time. She plays with friends, her uncle, and her brother at home. Next week the coach is holding tryouts.

2. **Which sentence tells what most likely happens next?**

   ○ A. Doris will decide to stay home.

   ○ B. Doris will try out for the team.

   ○ C. Doris will ask her brother to try out.

Practice Page 33

Name_____ Date_____

Read each paragraph. Then fill in the bubble that best answers each question.

Old Money

What happens to dollar bills when they get old and need replacing? For many years worn-out bills were shredded and dumped into the ground. It was a huge job. In recent years, old bills have begun to be recycled. U.S. paper money is made with cotton, so it is very strong. One company now makes roof tiles from shredded bills. Another company is trying to make fake fireplace logs.

1. **Which sentence tells what most likely happens next?**

   ○ A. Paper money will no longer be replaced.

   ○ B. Shredded bills will be recycled in more ways.

   ○ C. People will start spending shredded money.

Meet Irv

Irv enjoys trying new things. He is always willing to taste new foods. He likes knowing how to do the latest dances. Today Irv is trying to learn how to rollerblade. It doesn't bother him when his friends laugh at his wobbly steps. Ooops! Irv just tripped and fell on his face.

2. **Which sentence tells what most likely happens next?**

   ○ A. Irv will give up and go home.

   ○ B. Irv will get up and try again.

   ○ C. Irv will hide from his friends.

Practice Page 34 Name_____ Date_____

Read each paragraph. Then fill in the bubble
that best answers each question.

Catalog Houses

In the early 1900s many people bought their houses from a catalog. They chose the model they wanted and filled out an order form. Then the catalog company sent the house parts by train. A truck took the parts from the railroad station to the building site. The company also sent carpenters and other workers to put the house together. It took about two months.

1. **Which sentence tells what most likely happens next?**

   ○ A. The new owners will move in.

   ○ B. The new owners will sell the house.

   ○ C. The company will buy the house.

The Forgotten Panda

Each morning Gail walks her little sister to school. She holds her hand and makes sure Carol gets to the kindergarten room safely. Today Carol is crying. She is upset because she forgot her panda for show-and-tell. Gail can't get her sister to stop crying.

2. **Which sentence tells what most likely happens next?**

   ○ A. Gail will send Carol home to get the panda.

   ○ B. Gail will leave Carol on the sidewalk crying.

   ○ C. Gail will take Carol home to get the panda.

Practice Page 35

Name_____ Date_____

Read each paragraph. Then fill in the bubble
that best answers each question.

Album Quilts

Long ago many pioneer families
moved west. Sometimes their
friends gave them a good-bye party.
Before the party, people would
get together and plan a special
quilt. This was called an album
quilt. The quilt was a way for
the pioneers to remember their
friends. A different friend made
each block of the quilt. Each
block was signed by its maker.

1. **Which sentence tells what most
   likely happens next?**
   - A. The quilt-makers will decide to
     sell the quilt.
   - B. The family will trade the quilt
     for other supplies.
   - C. The quilt will be given to the
     family at the party.

Growing Pains

The town of Woodlands was
growing. Some parts of the town
had growing pains. The place where
Reed Street crossed Broad Street was
becoming dangerous. As more cars
used these roads, there were more
accidents. So the town decided to put
up a traffic light.

2. **Which sentence tells what
   most likely happens next?**
   - A. The number of accidents
     will go down.
   - B. More people will begin
     riding bikes.
   - C. The number of accidents
     will increase.

Assessment 1

Name_____ Date_____

Read the paragraph. Then answer the question.

New Things

The White House is where the U.S. president lives. Life in this building has changed over time. The White House got its first telephone in 1879. It got electric lights in 1891. An indoor swimming pool was added in 1942. The White House got its first fire alarm in 1965. After that came other new inventions such as computers and cell phones.

1. Make a prediction. What do you think the White House will get next?

_____

_____

Study the pictures. Then answer the questions.

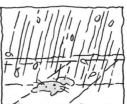

2. What will happen to the girl's drawing when the rain stops?

_____

3. Why do you think so?

_____

Assessment 2   Name_____   Date_____

Read the paragraph. Then answer the question.

Watch Out for Hailstones

Sometimes raindrops turn into hailstones. This usually happens in the summer. The raindrops get whipped around in cold clouds. They turn into bits of ice. The more the icy rain is tossed around, the bigger the layers of ice get. Hailstones can get as big as tennis balls. And they can do a lot of damage! When farmers see hailstones, they know trouble is right behind.

1. Make a prediction. What do you think will happen to the farmers' crops?

_____

Study the pictures. Then answer the questions.

2. What will the boy do when the bus arrives?

_____

3. Why do you think so?

_____

Assessment 3

Name_____

Date_____

Read the paragraph. Then answer the question.

A Colorful Story

People in a big city complained that their streets weren't being sanded in snowstorms. So the city started adding a green tint to the sand to show that it was there. Building owners also began using colored tints to melt snow and ice on their sidewalks. The streets looked like rainbows when it snowed. But not everyone was happy to get colored sand on their feet.

1. Make a prediction. What do you think will happen when people go indoors?

_____

Study the pictures. Then answer the questions.

2. What will the dog do next?

_____

3. Why do you think so?

_____

Student Record Sheet

Name _____ Date _____

Date	Practice Page # _____	Number Correct	Comments

Answers

Page 5:
1. He liked it a lot.
2. He was sorry it ended.
3. He thought the author did a great job.
4. He might look for the same author.
5. He had just a read a book by this author that he liked.
6. Answers will vary.

Page 8:
1. B
2. C
3. B
4. A
5. C
6. B
7. A
8. B

Page 9:
1. C
2. B

Page 10:
1. A
2. C

Page 11:
1. B
2. B

Page 12:
1. C
2. A

Page 13:
1. B
2. B

Page 14:
1. A
2. A

Page 15:
1. C
2. C

Page 16:
1. A
2. B

Page 17:
1. C
2. A

Page 18:
1. B
2. A

Page 19:
1. B
2. B

Page 20:
1. B
2. C

Page 21:
1. A
2. A

Page 22:
1. C
2. B

Page 23:
1. A
2. C

Page 24:
1. A
2. C

Page 25:
1. C
2. C

Page 26:
1. B
2. B

Page 27:
1. A
2. A

Page 28:
1. C
2. B

Page 29:
1. B
2. A

Page 30:
1. A
2. B

Page 31:
1. C
2. B

Page 32:
1. B
2. B

Page 33:
1. C
2. A

Page 34:
1. C
2. C

Page 35:
1. A
2. A

Page 36:
1. B
2. C

Page 37:
1. B
2. A

Page 38:
1. C
2. B

Page 39:
1. C
2. C

Page 40:
1. A
2. B

Page 41:
1. B
2. B

Page 42:
1. A
2. C

Page 43:
1. C
2. A

Page 44:
1. Possible answers: The White House will keep getting new inventions.

2. It will fade away.

3. The rain will wash it away.

Page 45:
1. Possible answers: The crops will be ruined.

2. He will get on the bus.

3. He has been waiting for the bus.

Page 46:
1. Possible answers: They will get colored sand on floors and rugs.

2. He will probably bark.

3. He can't climb the tree to get the cat.

SCHOLASTIC

From the Editors at Scholastic Teaching Resources

Dear Reader,

We're always delighted when teachers say, "Your books are the ones we use . . . the ones that go to school with us for a day's work . . . the ones that go home with us to help in planning. . . ."

Your comments tell us that our books work for you—supporting you in your daily planning and long-range goals, helping you bring fresh ideas into your classroom, and keeping you up to date with the latest trends in education. In fact, many Scholastic Teaching Resources are written by teachers, like you, who work in schools every day.

If you have an idea for a book you believe could help other teachers in any grade from PreK–8, please let us know! Send us a letter that includes your name, address, phone number, and the grade you teach; a table of contents; and a sample chapter or activities to:

Manuscript Editor
Scholastic Teaching Resources
557 Broadway
New York, NY 10012

Please understand that because of the large volume of interesting teacher ideas we receive, we will not be able to return your material. Be sure to keep the original and send us a copy. If we think your material might be a good fit for us, we will contact you.

—The Editors

Teaching *Resources*

READING PASSAGES
That Build Comprehension
Predicting

...nts the repeated practice they need to master the reading skill of ...edictions, and succeed on tests! Each of the 35 reproducible pages ...nterest fiction and nonfiction reading passages with bubble-test ...ons that target this essential reading comprehension skill. Flexible ...e—in school or at home—the book also includes model lessons, ...—and post-assessments, and an answer key.

Look for the other great books in this series:

Reading Passages That Build Comprehension: Fact & Opinion
Grades 2–3
ISBN: 0-439-55422-5

Reading Passages That Build Comprehension: Main Idea & Details
Grades 2–3
ISBN: 0-439-55425-X

Reading Passages That Build Comprehension: Inference
Grades 2–3
ISBN: 0-439-55424-1

Reading Passages That Build Comprehension: Context Clues
Grades 2–3
ISBN: 0-439-55426-8

Reading Passages That Build Comprehension: Compare & Contrast
Grades 2–3
ISBN: 0-439-55427-6

Teaching Resources

$10.99 U.S./$14.99 CAN.

ISBN-13: 978-0-439-55423-7
ISBN-10: 0-439-55423-3

51099>
EAN
9 780439 554237

SCHOLASTIC
The Most Trusted Name In Learning®

www.scholastic.com